DONCASTER
TROLLEYBUSES

Colin Barker

Series editor Robert J Harley

MP Middleton Press

Published March 2011

ISBN 978 1 906008 92 5

© Middleton Press, 2011

Design Deborah Esher

Published by
> *Middleton Press*
> *Easebourne Lane*
> *Midhurst*
> *West Sussex*
> *GU29 9AZ*

Tel: 01730 813169
Fax: 01730 812601
Email: info@middletonpress.co.uk
www.middletonpress.co.uk

Printed in the United Kingdom by Henry Ling Limited, at the Dorset Press, Dorchester, DT1 1HD

CONTENTS

INTRODUCTION
AND ACKNOWLEDGMENTS

Following the publication of my book on Mexborough and Swinton for this series, I contemplated what might have been if the 2.8 mile (4.5km) connection had been made with the Doncaster Corporation trolleybus system. If it had been constructed between Conisbrough Low on the Mexborough system and Balby, a 12.5 mile (20.1km) indirect route between Doncaster and Rotherham would have been a possibility. These thoughts drew me towards completing this book on the Doncaster system.

The system has provided plenty of interest with its pre war three axled fleet, lack of town centre overhead turnouts and junctions, second hand vehicles fitted with new replacement bodies, with some in turn being fitted to motorbus chassis.

This book is not intended to be a detailed history of the system, but more a pictorial illustration of a period in the town's public transport history depicting the vehicles and the routes they served. The coverage starts with the north west route to Bentley and the remainder are detailed working round the town in a clockwise direction.

I am indebted to those who have generously agreed to the use of their photographs, either as the photographer, collection holder or copyright owner and due accreditation has been given with each view. There are a few views where I have not been able to trace the source but I hope the originators feel that their choice of subject or location has greatly enhanced the book's content for the reader.

Having never seen the Doncaster system in operation, I have been helped by Geoff Warnes and Peter Tuffrey, whose local knowledge has been invaluable. They also kindly read through the first draft manuscript, together with Roger Holmes and Richard Buckley; all provided many constructive suggestions. Roger Smith provided the map with Richard Buckley's agreement, the line drawings were by Terry Russell, tickets provided by Eric Old and the timetables/fare charts were via the Omnibus Society's Walsall library. Last but not least, a big thank you to my wife Maureen for her continued help and support, particularly in helping with research visits to Doncaster, and use of her computer skills to format the final version.

HISTORICAL AND GEOGRAPHICAL BACKGROUND

Doncaster is situated in South Yorkshire astride the River Don. The earliest settlement was when a fort was created by the Romans at the river crossing that was later called Danum, from which the word Don is derived. When the Saxons arrived in South Yorkshire their name for the fort was Dona Ceastre (camp on the Don). Over time a village grew near the fort that carried the name Doncaster; this developed into a small busy market town, which was granted a charter by Richard 1 in the 12th century. The town continued to grow despite outbreaks of the plague and typhoid in the 16th and 17th centuries.

The numerous town centre streets carrying the word Gate in the title have their origins from the Danish word Gata that means street. Craftsmen and tradesmen professions were added before the word; for example Baxtergate, where baxter was an early word for a baker.

Doncaster Racecourse is one of the oldest in the country, and home of the world famous St Leger, which was first held in 1776.

Doncaster lies on the north/south route between London and York and was an important stopping point for stagecoaches, hence the many hostelries catering for this daily trade. In 1850, the London to York railway was completed with a station in the town. Three years later the Great Northern Railway (GNR) sited its workshops in the town leading to the complex becoming the major employer in the area. This development, plus the discovery of coal in the surrounding areas at the turn of the century, and the use of the river and canals for transportation, changed this agricultural market town into a major manufacturing centre with a variety of industries. These declined, particularly in the case of coal, in the second half of the 20th century.

In the early part of the 20th century, the borough boundaries were extended to include the surrounding areas of Hexthorpe, Wheatley and Balby. The town became a County Borough in 1927 and further boundary extensions were implemented in 1936. Today it forms part of the Metropolitan Borough of Doncaster with a population of circa 286,000 when the surrounding areas are included.

PUBLIC TRANSPORT HISTORY

The growth of industry in Doncaster, particularly the opening of the GNR workshops and the development of coalmines in the area, led to the need for some form of public transport to move the population to and from their place of work.

Early proposals for a tramway in 1878 failed, as did a line to Balby in 1895. From 1887, horse bus services began to be introduced by some local businesses to convey passengers from outlaying areas. The large grocery store of Hodgson and Hepworth was one of these, together with J G Steadman who became a well known taxi operator.

In 1898, the British Electric Traction Company Limited (BET) proposed plans for electric tram routes to Avenue Road, Balby, Bentley and Hexthorpe. Doncaster council had already decided to build an electric power station and could see that an electric tramway would provide a good base load for the generator, so presented their own proposals. They were similar to that of the BET, but also included the Hyde Park and Racecourse routes, and were submitted under the 1896 Light Railway Act. An Order was granted to the council, but it stipulated that the Bentley route would have to be remote from the rest of the system pending a bridge being built over the main north/south railway line to replace the level crossing.

There was a two year delay before construction commenced, with the first two routes to Bentley and Hexthorpe opening on 2nd June 1902; all the proposed routes were operational by January 1903. Further routes were opened to Beckett Road and Oxford Road in late 1903, and an extension of the Balby route to Warmsworth in 1915. Finally, a new route to Brodsworth was opened in 1916 to serve the growing coal mining activity in the area. Two depots were built, the main one being in Greyfriars Road, plus a small facility on the isolated Bentley route. Fifteen cars were initially ordered for the opening of the system.

Motor buses began to be introduced in 1922. The route to Rossington used this form of vehicle, notwithstanding that ten new trams had been ordered, which could not be cancelled, and a depot extension built to house them. As with all tramway systems, vehicles and infrastructure had deteriorated during the 1914-1918 war due to a shortage of materials and skilled labour. This was exacerbated by the increase in private motorbus competition after the war. In 1925, motorbuses were used to Wheatley Hills via Avenue Road, replacing the tram route to the latter. The Oxford Road tram route had been closed earlier in 1907 due to lack of revenue.

The Bentley route was closed in 1928 when the local councils wanted to relay the road to a higher level. This, coupled with the many earlier complaints regarding the condition of the track, turned thoughts to the use of trolleybuses as a replacement. General powers to run trolleybuses had been obtained under the Doncaster Corporation Act of 1926, with the systems in Leeds and Bradford having been inspected as early as 1912.

The route was converted to trolleybuses with a single line extension loop around Bentley New Village, which began on 22nd August 1928. An extension through to Toll Bar was authorised but never built. There were proposals to run trolleybuses to other surrounding mining villages but only the one to Edlington was authorised, although operated by motor buses when the route opened. Other conversions quickly followed with the route to Hexthorpe, servicing the railway workshops, opening on 1st July 1929, and along Beckett Road as far as Wentworth Road on 31st July 1929; the latter route was extended twice in 1941 and 1958.

The Hyde Park route was converted on the 16th January 1930, quickly followed by that to the Racecourse three months later, thus providing clockwise and anti-clockwise circular routes from the town centre. Trolleybuses replaced the motor buses on the Wheatley Hills route on the 4th March 1931, terminating at the Wheatley Hotel; the route was extended in 1958. Finally, the Balby route was converted on the 26th July 1931, with a reverser terminus off the main road in Cedar Road; this was replaced by a short extension in 1942 along the main road to Barrel Lane.

All pre war deliveries were three axle vehicles, with the initial supply coming from Garrett and Karrier-Clough with Roe bodies. The first Garrett, delivered in April 1928, was used on driver training on the Racecourse route using a trailing skate in the tram track for the electrical negative return. Apart from one Bristol, all subsequent pre war deliveries were of Karrier-Clough or Karrier manufacture and mounted with Roe bodies.

The demands of the 1939-1945 war, plus the age of the early vehicles, resulted in nine utility Karriers being delivered between 1943 and 1945. After the war, six relatively new BUT trolleybuses were purchased from Darlington Corporation in 1952 and subsequently sold to Bradford City Transport, after their withdrawal by Doncaster in 1959.

After a change in general manager, an astute policy of purchasing second hand trolleybuses after other system closures was pursued, with the chassis being overhauled and new higher capacity bodies fitted. In turn, some of the bodies were adapted to fit motor bus chassis after the trolleybuses were eventually withdrawn.

Following the nationalisation of the electricity industry in 1947, municipal generated supplies ended with subsequent cost increases. The decision of London Transport, and a number of other municipal operators, to abandon trolleybuses reduced the requirement for overhead equipment and fittings, with the main UK supplier withdrawing from the market. The range of trolleybus chassis also drastically reduced. These factors, plus the need to access new housing estates and the advent of new road schemes, resulted in the rapid decline in trolleybus systems, although Doncaster took advantage of this with its second hand purchases and rebodying.

The Bentley route was the first to close, with the system route mileage standing at a maximum of 13 miles (20.9 km) before closure, due to the reconstruction of Mill Bridge; the service ceased on 12th February 1956. The main closure programme began in December 1961 with the Hyde Park route, (other than for race day specials), followed by Hexthorpe, Balby and Wheatley Hills in March, September and December 1962. The Racecourse route closed in October 1963 and the final closure came with Beckett Road on 14th December 1963, with 375 carrying out the final duty. So ended 61½ years of electrically powered public transport, with the trolleybuses contributing

35½ years. 375 passed to the Doncaster Omnibus and Light Railway Society and is held at the Trolleybus Museum at Sandtoft, North Lincolnshire.

One final item of interest was a prototype trolleybus commissioned by the South Yorkshire Passenger Transport Executive (PTE), which was revealed in September 1985. Based on a standard front entrance motorbus, it was fitted with an electric motor, control equipment and booms and ran along a mile of test overhead adjacent to the racecourse. It had been hoped to re-introduce trolleybuses in Doncaster and Rotherham, but de-regulation of the bus industry resulted in the project proceeding no further. This vehicle can also be seen at Sandtoft.

Route Numbers

1	Bentley	5	Beckett Road	Route numbers were
3	Hexthorpe	6	Racecourse / Hyde Park circulars	eventually abandoned
4	Wheatley Hills	10	Balby	

Abbreviations

BET   British Electric Traction Company Limited (Transport operating company)
BUT   British United Traction (Trolleybus chassis manufacturer)
GNR   Great Northern Railway
NTA   National Trolleybus Association
OTA   Online Transport Archive
PTE   Passenger Transport Executive
UK   United Kingdom

Liveries

Initial	Predominantly off white with maroon relief
Pre War	Maroon with three off white bands and silver roof
Post War 1	Crimson Lake (also quoted as Dark Red) with three white bands
Post War 2	Red with one white band above lower windows

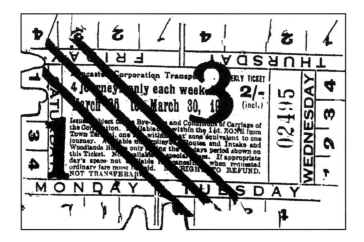

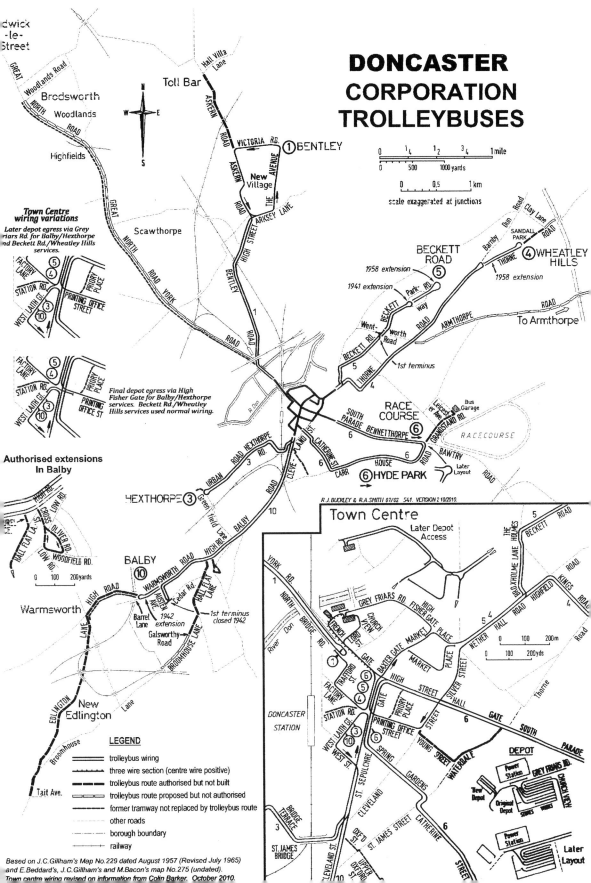

DONCASTER
CORPORATION
TROLLEYBUSES

dwick
-le-
Street

Toll Bar

Brodsworth

Woodlands Road

NORTH ROAD

Woodlands

Highfields

GREAT

Hall Villa Lane

ASKERN ROAD

VICTORIA RD. ① BENTLEY

New Village

THE AVENUE

ASKERN ROAD

ARKSEY LANE

HIGH STREET

BENTLEY ROAD

Scawthorpe

GREAT NORTH ROAD

YORK ROAD

**Town Centre
wiring variations**

*Later depot egress via Grey
riars Rd. for Balby/Hexthorpe
and Beckett Rd./Wheatley Hills
services.*

FACTORY LANE
⑤
④
STATION RD.
③
WEST LAITH G.
⑩
PRINTING OFFICE STREET
PRIORY PLACE

FACTORY LANE
⑤
④
STATION RD.
③
WEST LAITH G.
⑩
PRINTING OFFICE ST.
PRIORY PLACE

*Final depot egress via High
Fisher Gate for Balby/Hexthorpe
services. Beckett Rd./Wheatley
Hills services used normal wiring.*

R. Don

scale exaggerated at junctions

0   1/4   1/2   3/4   1 mile
0   500   1000 yards
0   0.5   1 km

Don Road
Clay Lane

SANDALL PARK

Barnby

THORNE

BECKETT ROAD ⑤

1958 extension

1941 extension

Park Rd.

way

Went- worth Road

BECKETT RD.

THORNE RD.

ARMTHORPE ROAD

1st terminus

④ WHEATLEY HILLS

1958 extension

ROAD

To Armthorpe

**Authorised extensions
In Balby**

HALL FLAT LA.
HIGH RD.
CROSS
OLIVER RD.
LOW RD.
WOODFIELD RD.

HEXTHORPE ③

URBAN ROAD

HEXTHORPE RD.

Green field

0   100   200 yards

BALBY ⑩

WARMSWORTH ROAD

HIGH RD.

AUSTEN AVE.

Cedar Rd.

HALL FLAT LANE

Warmsworth

HIGH ROAD

LANE

Barrel Lane

1942 extension

Galsworthy Road

BROOMHOUSE LANE

LANE

EDLINGTON LANE

New Edlington

Broomhouse

Tait Ave.

CLEVELAND ST.

CATHERINE ST.

SOUTH PARADE

CARR HOUSE ROAD

⑥ HYDE PARK

BENNETTHORPE

RACE COURSE ⑥

GRANDSTAND RD.

Leicester Ave.

Bus Garage

RACECOURSE

BAWTRY ROAD

Later Layout

*1st terminus
closed 1942*

R. J. BUCKLEY & R. A. SMITH 07/02 541. VERSION 2 10/2010.

Town Centre

Later Depot Access

YORK RD.

NORTH BRIDGE RD.

River Don

DONCASTER STATION

GREY FRIARS RD.

FRENCH GATE

LORD ST.

TRAFFORD ST.

FACTORY LANE

STATION RD.

WEST LAITH G.

WEST ST.

HIGH FISHER GATE

CHURCH VIEW

BAXTER GATE

MARKET

PRINTING OFFICE STREET

PRIORY PLACE

SPRING GARDENS

YOUNG STREET

SPURN

HIGH STREET

MARKET PLACE

SILVER STREET

NETHER HALL ROAD

HALL GATE

WATERDALE

ST. SEPULCHRE

CLEVELAND

ST. JAMES STREET

BRIDGE TERRACE

ST. JAMES BRIDGE

CLEVELAND ST.

UPPER OXFORD ST.

OXFD. ST.

CATHERINE

THE HOLMES

BECKETT ROAD

BROXHOLME LANE

HIGHFIELD ROAD

KINGS ROAD

Thorne

SOUTH PARADE

0   100   200m
0   100   200yds

GATE

DEPOT

Power Station

GREY FRIARS RD.

CHURCH VIEW

New Depot

Original Depot

STORES   WIRES

Power Station

Later Layout

LEGEND

trolleybus wiring
three wire section (centre wire positive)
trolleybus route authorised but not built
trolleybus route proposed but not authorised
former tramway not replaced by trolleybus route
other roads
borough boundary
railway

Based on J.C.Gillham's Map No.229 dated August 1957 (Revised July 1965)
and E.Beddard's, J.C.Gillham's and M.Bacon's map No.275 (undated).
Town centre wiring revised on information from Colin Barker. October 2010.

TRAMS TO TROLLEYBUSES

1. The first trolleybus, namely Garrett 1, is seen here on trade plates undergoing trials on the Racecourse route in 1928. Only one boom is being used, which is connected to the single positive tram overhead, with the negative connection via a towed trailing skate in the tram track. The vehicle was used for initial driver training in 1928, and again at the end of its life in the period 1936 to 1938. An inspector stands next to Car 7, one of the batch that opened the system (originally open topped), which was withdrawn in 1930. The motorman is perhaps looking forward to the weather protection the trolleybus will provide after his training on the new type of vehicle.
(P Tuffrey collection)

2. Karrier-Clough E6 24 and Car 41 were photographed outside the Doncaster and District Steam Laundry in Balby Road sometime between March 1931, when the trolleybus entered service, and 1933 when the tram was withdrawn. Note the tram passing loop, and the overhead wiring suspended from separate bracket arms on each side of the road. Car 41 was from the last batch of trams delivered in 1920, and was burnt out on the Brodsworth route in 1933 following an electrical fault. The unusual centre grooved tram track can be seen in the foreground.
(Author's collection)

BENTLEY

3. The Bentley route was the first to be converted to trolleybuses, opening on 22nd August 1928. Karrier W 370 stands in Factory Lane, about to be overtaken by a Rotherham single deck motorbus, which is on a fisherman's special. The single set of overhead wiring from St Sepulchre Gate on the left, was used by vehicles travelling from the depot to take up service for Bentley, and also the return journey at the end of the working day. The destination indicator has yet to be changed. 370, delivered in 1943, received a chassis overhaul and a new Roe body, re-entering service during 1958. The modern Co-op building can be seen behind the Rotherham vehicle, with their older premises to the right; note the rather precarious ladder on the roof of the latter. (G Warnes)

← 4. This unidentified Karrier E6 has just left Factory Lane and turned right into Trafford Street. At the end of this thoroughfare, it will turn left into French Gate to reach North Bridge for the beginning of the Bentley service. This view was taken in late December 1955, a few weeks before the route closed on 12th February 1956. (G Warnes)

← 5. Vehicles starting their duty would pick up passengers outside the Brown Cow public house, which was opposite the small bus station used as the town terminus for the rest of the day. Karrier E6 355 waits to start its run to Bentley village under two sets of overhead wiring. That nearest the pavement is the single wiring from St. Sepulchre Gate seen in the previous views; to take up service the booms had to be transferred to the wiring being used by 355. A gentleman can be seen leaving the public toilet; this facility was very convenient for male crew members. (A D Packer)

6. Inbound vehicles used the small bus station perched above French Gate on the North Bridge approach and Karrier-Clough E6 5 is seen on layover before returning to Bentley. Note the lower panels have been painted maroon as opposed to the original off white; presumably the latter proving impracticable in service. Also note the two types of window, with horizontal opening on the top deck and vertical on the lower. To the rear is a Bullock Leyland motorbus destined for Selby and York. (Omnibus Society)

7. A rear view of Karrier E6 341 in a busy North Bridge bus station. The rear destination indicator can be seen in the upper window and the boom retainer has inward facing hooks. 341 was one of six into service over the 1935 year end, which were the last to have the lower deck partitioned into smoking and non smoking. They were also the last to be fitted with rear towing hooks, which can be seen here on each side of the vehicle registration number. (C Routh)

8. Immaculate BUT 381 (ex Darlington 71) waits on stand at North Bridge with the system's power station chimney in the background. It must have been a warm day when the photograph was taken with windscreen and window vents open. 381 was one of six trolleybuses purchased from Darlington Corporation in 1952, which were subsequently sold on to Bradford City Transport in 1960, where five were rebodied. It became Bradford 833, being eventually withdrawn in 1971. The white window surround livery used here after purchase from Darlington, was to see two further changes on some of the batch.
(R F Mack/J Fozard copyright)

9. When coming off service vehicles had to make a dangerous manoeuvre to return to the depot, which BUT 380 (ex Darlington 70) is just about to start. The booms are down and the driver has his hand out of the side window to indicate he is about to cross to the opposite side of the road (freewheeling down the incline) to stop outside the Brown Cow public house. Remember that when this photograph was taken this was the busy A1 trunk road as indicated by the traffic. Having reached this position the booms would be raised to gain the depot wiring (see Picture 5) and 380 will then travel counter flow on the wrong side of the road a short distance before turning right into Trafford Street on the single wiring described earlier. It is suggested some drivers would commence the move as indicated and then sweep through 180 degrees into lower French Gate to finish up under depot wiring, although this would have been extremely difficult. Note the differing liveries on the ex Darlington vehicles in this view. (G Warnes)

← 10. At the end of a return trip from Bentley BUT 379 (ex Darlington 69) enters the small bus station on the town side of North Bridge; after subsequent resale and a new body this vehicle became Bradford 832. The white window surrounds enhanced the vehicle's appearance compared with later liveries. Note the Baby Austin on the left. (C Carter)

← 11. BUT 382 (ex Darlington 72) is seen passing underneath the railway bridge, which carried a goods avoiding line over the bottom end of Bentley Road, and is returning to town having completed a short working to Playfairs Corner. The bridge still exists over the traffic island where the A19 joins the A638, and was the only under bridge on the system. The Esso tiger takes second place to the Guinness pint.
(G Warnes)

12. Having left the under bridge on the outward journey, BUT 382 (ex Darlington 72) is about to cross the flood arches at the bottom of Bentley Road and pass under a section insulator/feeder. Section insulators were inserted into the overhead approximately every half-mile to ensure a fault in one section could be isolated from those adjacent. It was usually the place where electric power was fed to the overhead from sub stations as illustrated here. The shop in the centre of the view is now a private residence.
(G Warnes)

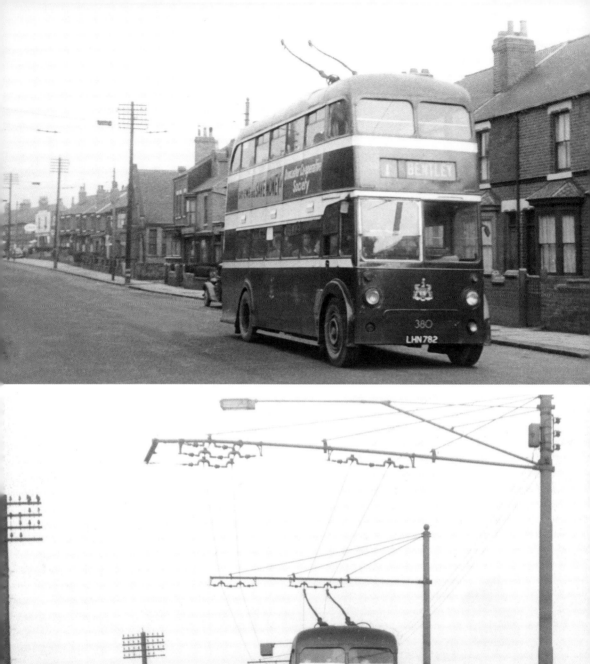

← 13. BUT 380 (ex Darlington 70) is seen returning to town along a deserted Bentley Road. 380 was one of two that were painted with the three white band format before the whole batch were finished in the final single white band livery in 1956/57. One feature in the scene, not generally seen today, are the substantial telegraph poles. (G Warnes)

← 14. BUT 380 (ex Darlington 70) has left Bentley High Street and crosses the railway bridge into Bentley Road whilst returning to town, as the sun reflects on the driver's windscreen. The overhead is carried by bracket arms with both 18" (457mm) and 24" (610mm) spacing. 380 became Bradford 832 on subsequent sale and re-bodying. To the left the railway line leads towards Adwick le Street and Wakefield to the north west; the view dates from December 1955. (G Warnes)

15. Karrier E6 348 climbs Bentley High Street to approach the bridge seen in the previous picture in September 1955, with the Bentley parish church of St Peter as the backdrop. Sodium street lighting is mounted from the traction standard. (G Warnes)

← 16. Garrett 3, from the first 1928 trolleybus deliveries, moves towards the stop on the right in Bentley Road opposite Church Street, with a waiting lady dressed in late 1920s fashion. The white band on the traction standard identifies the stop, a practice continued throughout the life of the system. This one has the wording "Car Stop" on the band that, together with the covered tram track in the centre of the road, reflects the earlier form of public transport on this route. Looking towards Bentley village, the building behind the Garrett is the Druids Arms now renamed as "Druids at Bentley" (P Tuffrey collection)

← 17. A smart youth waits to alight from Karrier E6 347 at Playfairs Corner in July 1955 as it turns into the beginning of the single line loop around Bentley village. After stopping it will travel a short distance along Arksey Lane before turning left into The Avenue. The overhead wiring to the left, tied off to the traction standard, allowed vehicles on a Playfairs short working to reverse around the corner ready for the return trip to town; this manoeuvre required the booms to be changed onto the stub wiring. (G Warnes)

18. BUT 380 (ex Darlington 70) reverses around Playfairs Corner into Askern Road using the wiring described in the previous picture. When the move is completed, booms will be transferred to the wiring seen top right, and on the return towards town 380 will cross over the wiring into Arksey Lane. The bamboo retrieval pole can just be seen hanging from the right hand boom ready to carry out the transfer. The tube for housing the retrieval pole can be seen below the rear panel. (G Warnes)

19. Karrier E6 340 has travelled along the single loop and is seen here on stand in The Avenue on what appears to be a very warm day in May 1952. The white band on the traction standard identifies the stop as indicated earlier. This vehicle entered service in 1936 and lasted until 1954. (R Marshall)

20. After travelling along The Avenue, vehicles turned left into Victoria Road and thence to Askern Road. Here BUT 383 (ex Darlington 73) turns into Askern Road (A19) ready to travel along the last leg of the loop in April 1955. An extension to Toll Bar, along the road to the left, was authorised but never built. The property on the left has been demolished and replaced with modern apartments. The Bentley pit head gear can just be seen on the central distant skyline. (R K Blencowe collection)

21. BUT 381 (ex Darlington 71) moves along Askern Road in September 1954 on the last leg of the loop under 18" (457mm) spaced overhead wiring and closely followed by two motorcyclists. This vehicle was withdrawn early after an accident in 1959 before being sold to Bradford. On the right is the Rostholme Social Club, previously a Working Mens' Club. (G Warnes)

22. Karrier E6 346 completes the Bentley loop and leaves Askern Road to enter Bentley High Street at Playfairs Corner in July 1955. It is about to pass under the diamond crossover, which carried the wiring from the High Street on the right into Arksey Lane at the beginning of the loop (see Picture 17). (G Warnes)

BECKETT ROAD AND WHEATLEY HILLS
Town Centre to Nether Hall Road

23. We are now in St Sepulchre Gate, where the town centre stands for both routes were located. On departure, they shared common wiring for the first part of their outward journeys and the latter part of the return to the town centre. Karrier E6 347 waits for departure to Beckett Road under the central set of overhead leading from Printing Office Street; wiring on the left was for the Racecourse route leading from Spring Gardens. The wiring on the right was used by Bentley trolleybuses taking up service via French Gate (travelling right to left on the wrong side of the road) and on return to depot, plus those taking up service to the Balby/ Hexthorpe stands in West Laith Gate. It was also used by Beckett Road and Wheatley Hills vehicles entering service as indicated in the next caption. These arrangements changed later when depot access was via High Fisher Gate (see Picture 26). (D A Jones)

➔ 24. One of the three Brush bodied utility Karrier Ws, namely 373 (rebodied in 1954), awaits departure to Wheatley Hills from outside the Hodgson and Hepworth store. This business provided horse drawn transport from surrounding areas to encourage trade before the introduction of trams. The only overhead turnout junction in the town centre can be seen top left. The right hand branch for the Bentley route curves round into Factory Lane, whilst the left hand wiring provided egress from the depot via French Gate to the Balby/ Hexthorpe stands in West Laith Gate, where vehicles can be seen in the distance. Vehicles entering service for Beckett Road and Wheatley Hills would enter West Laith Gate, change booms and reverse around the corner into St Sepulchre Gate, and after a further boom change, move across to their stand using Racecourse wiring. Finally, booms would be transferred to their own route wiring. These arrangements changed in later years as indicated in the previous caption. (D F Parker)

25. Karrier W 370, with original Park Royal utility bodywork, waits at the Wheatley Hills stand, with the vehicle in front reflecting on the nearside windscreen. Behind the Fordson van is the Harry Jacobs Furniture Store, known locally as Jacobs Corner. Before the introduction of direct wiring into West Laith Gate, as indicated in the previous caption, vehicles taking up service had to travel all round the Racecourse route. On the left, a pre war Austin car is parked in front of a new post war Morris Minor. Does anyone locally recognise the gentleman on the right? (D A Jones)

← 26. Having left St Sepulchre Gate, vehicles for both routes travelled along Baxter Gate to reach the Market Place, where rebodied Sunbeam W 397 (ex Mexborough and Swinton 5), destined for Beckett Road, passes cautiously through the shopping crowds in September 1961. In the background, to the rear of 397 is High Fisher Gate, which was wired for depot access in later years to replace the earlier French Gate route. The wiring on the right was from High Fisher Gate for vehicles taking up service in the town centre; unconnected overhead leading into High Fisher Gate from Baxter Gate on the left, was for vehicles returning to depot, which can just be seen adjacent to Franklin's corner shop. (A D Packer)

← 27. Rebodied Sunbeam W 351 (ex Pontypridd 10) has left the Market Place and now moves along the short length of Sunny Bar before entering Nether Hall Road, with the Market Hall/Corn Exchange in the background. The wiring on the left led into Silver Street allowing vehicles leaving the depot via High Fisher Gate to reach stands in St Sepulchre Gate. On the left, is an Austin A40 car in front of a Morris Minor van. After withdrawal in 1962 the body of 351 was adapted to fit Daimler motorbus 170. (R F Mack/J Fozard copyright)

28. This view was taken at the town end of Nether Hall Road, near the junction with Silver Street, and depicts Karrier E6 46 or 48 (before renumbering) moving along the centre of the road between parked vehicles. A photograph exists of trolleybus campaigner Stanley King standing outside the butcher's shop of the same name on the right, although there is no family connection. The car in the foreground is a Triumph Dolomite saloon. (P Tuffrey collection)

Beckett Road

29. We now reach the point where the two routes part company. Rebodied Sunbeam W 388 (ex Southend 134) on the Beckett Road route turns out of Nether Hall Road into Broxholme Lane in April 1962. On the left, a vehicle on the Wheatley Hills route travels back to the town centre. Note the advertisement for Easter road races at Cadwell, with the traction standard behind carrying the switch equipment for the automatic overhead turnout junction. The substantial Methodist church in the background has been converted into an apartment complex called Concorde Mews.
(C Routh)

30. Rebodied Karrier W 369, now carrying a Sunbeam badge, leaves The Holmes to enter Broxholme Lane near the junction with Kings Road on its return to the town centre. Many of the Karrier W rebodied trolleybuses also received Sunbeam badges. A discount motor accessories outlet now occupies the shops on the right and 369 is being followed by a Ford Thames Trader lorry. (R G H Simpson)

31. Victorian pallisaded housing on Beckett Road near Avenue Road forms the backdrop for rebodied Sunbeam W 353 (ex Mexborough and Swinton 14) as it travels towards town. Note the Triumph saloon on the extreme left plus the motorcycle and sidecar waiting to turn into Beckett Road. The latter was a familiar means of family transport before the growth of car ownership after the war. (V Nutton/Travel Lens Photographic)

← 32. The original trolleybus terminus was at the junction of Beckett Road and Wentworth Road, where a triangular reverser was installed. Karrier-Clough E6 18 waits to return to town having completed the reversing manoeuvre, with the crew posing accompanied by a young boy; perhaps one of the crew was a relation. The then Parish Hall can be seen in the background on the corner of Wentworth Road, which now houses the Doncaster Evangelical Church. (C Carter)

← 33. In 1941, the route was extended along Beckett Road to the junction with Parkway North/South. Karrier E6 356 moves round the terminal loop ready for the return journey. Typical post war local authority housing is supported by the obligatory row of shops in the background.
(R K Blencowe collection)

34. BUT 380 (ex Darlington 70), on a return trip to town, is seen outside the Astra cinema in Beckett Road. In many towns and cities, outlying cinemas were popular in the immediate post war period, but with the increase in television ownership their patronage declined. The Astra was no exception and a supermarket now occupies the site. When sold to Bradford, this vehicle was rebodied and became 832 in their fleet.
(R F Mack/J Fozard copyright)

35. In 1958, the route was extended a second time to the end of Beckett Road, and here two re-bodied Karrier Ws, 372 and 375, pass each other amongst three-storied housing stock adjacent to Parkway. 372, on the left, is making the return journey to the town centre. The destination indicator has not been changed after leaving the terminus and this practice applied on all routes. (G Warnes)

36. Re-bodied Sunbeam W 391 (ex Southend 137) has nearly reached the end of the Beckett Road route. Turning was along a single line around a pear shaped road that formed a convenient terminal loop, the start and finish of which can be seen in this view. The use of the long clamping ears, holding the overhead wires in the right foreground, was first seen by the author in Maidstone. Perhaps the new manager in 1953, Mr T Bamford, who came from Maidstone Corporation, brought their use to Doncaster. (C Carter)

37. Re-bodied Karrier W 375 waits on layover at the terminus of the Beckett Road route, with estate shops and flats as a backdrop. All of these buildings have been demolished to make way for a small bungalow development. The long wire clamping ears holding the overhead mentioned in the previous picture can also be seen in this view.
(V Nutton/Travel Lens Photographic)

Wheatley Hills

38. We now return to the junction of Nether Hall Road and Broxholme Lane to follow the Wheatley Hills route. Rebodied Sunbeam W 397 (ex Mexborough and Swinton 5) leaves Highfield Road and enters Nether Hall Road, with Beckett Road wiring curving left into Broxholme Lane. The location was one of two that had driver operated automatic overhead junction turnouts, the other being where the Balby and Hexthorpe routes diverged; originally they were hand operated by the conductor. The driver would take power from the overhead, against the resistance of the handbrake, as the positive boom passed under contacts on each side of the turnout. The first would operate a solenoid to change the direction of the turnout, and the second would restore it to its original position. This sequence was required for the Wheatley Hills route; trolleybuses on the Beckett Road route would ensure no power was being taken and coast over the first contact. Drivers bound for Wheatley Hills required skill to pass over the turnout and adjacent crossover, as each had a dead section in quick succession, with the second contact in-between. (C Carter)

39. Further along Highfield Road, there is a sharp right hand bend into Kings Road, as depicted in this view. Rebodied Karrier W 374 turns the corner out of Kings Road on a return trip to town, with the climb up to Thorne Road to the rear.
(V Nutton/Travel Lens Photographic)

40. At the top of the Kings Road incline, rebodied Sunbeam W 397 (ex Mexborough and Swinton 5) is about to turn into Thorne Road on an outward journey. It has turned out of Highfield Road at the bottom of the hill, with the landmark gasometer on the banks of the River Don in the distance. The white band on the traction standard again indicated a bus stop (C Carter)

41. The wide road and modern semi detached housing provide the backdrop for rebodied Karrier W 376 as it makes its way back to town along Thorne Road, near the Royal Infirmary. Initially, the Wheatley Hills destination blind was red, with some suggesting that it indicated the route passed the Royal Infirmary. A more likely explanation is that the block lettering of the Beckett Road and Wheatley Hills destinations were difficult to identify as vehicles approached, bearing in mind that they followed the same roads from the town centre; the change of colour solved the problem. However, the display of a red light at the front eventually became illegal. (V Nutton/Travel Lens Photographic)

42. The original terminus of the Wheatley Hills route was at the Y junction of Thorne Road and Barnby Dun Road, adjacent to the Wheatley Hotel. Rebodied Sunbeam W 396 (ex Mexborough and Swinton 4) waits in the lay-by, having travelled around the terminal circle. (Author's collection)

TROLLEY BUS ROUTE No. 4 — WHEATLEY HILLS

DONCASTER, St. Sepulchre Gate, WHEATLEY HILLS, Wheatley Hotel

SUNDAY		SATURDAY	
Depart St. Sepulchre Gate	Depart Wheatley Hotel	Depart St. Sepulchre Gate	Depart Wheatley Hotel
12 00 noon	12 15 p.m.	As Monday to Friday until	
12 15 p.m.	12 30	8 30 a.m.	8 45 a.m.
12 30	12 45	and every 5 mins. until	
and every 15 mins. until		5 00 p.m.	5 15 p.m.
2 00 p.m.	2 15 p.m.	5 06	5 21
2 07	2 22	and every 6 mins. until	
2 15	2 30	6 00 p.m.	6 15 p.m.
and every 7 and 8 mins. until		6 07	6 22
10 15 p.m.	10 30 p.m.	6 15	6 30
10 22	10 37	and every 7 and 8 mins. until	
10 30	10 45	10 45 p.m.	11 00 p.m.
		10 52	11 07
		11 00	11 15

MONDAY TO FRIDAY	
Depart St. Sepulchre Gate	Depart Wheatley Hotel
6 00 a.m.	6 15 a.m.
6 30	6 45
6 40	6 55
and every 10 mins. until	
7 50 a.m.	8 05 a.m.
8 00	8 15
and every 6 mins until	
7 30 p.m.	7 45 p.m.
7 37	7 52
7 45	8 00
and every 7 and 8 mins. until	
10 45 p.m.	11 00 p.m.
10 52	11 07
11 00	11 15

WHEATLEY HILLS ROUTE (No. 4).

Bk up						
Out	In					
1	1		Station Road			
2	—	1½	Sunny Bar			
	2	1½	1½	Kings Road (top)		
3	3	1½	1½	1½	New Infirmary	
4	4	2	1½	1½	1½	Wheatley Hotel

Timetable and Fare Chart 1950

43. In 1958, the route was extended a further ⅓ mile (0.53km) to the edge of Sandall Park; it only lasted a further four years until the closure of the system. A private part circle was built on the approach and a lay-by on the other side of the road. Both can be seen in this view, with rebodied Karrier W 352 (ex Pontypridd 11) in the lay-by waiting for the smartly dressed lady to board. A further extension along Thorne Road to near the junction with Clay Lane was authorised but never implemented.
(W A Camwell)

← 44. Having covered the two routes to their termini, we return to the town centre where returning trolleybuses from both routes shared a single loop to bring them back to St Sepulchre Gate. After leaving the double wiring at Nether Hall Road, vehicles turned left into Silver Street at the beginning of the loop. Karrier E6 347 is seen in Silver Street in September 1955 on a return trip from Beckett Road. The shop of Arnold Drury on the right appears to be selling horseflesh judging by the advertisement in the window, and the building behind 347 was originally the premises of Alfred Hall Ltd. (G Warnes)

← 45. Karrier-Clough E6 23, in original livery, continues along the single loop and is about to cross the dual wiring of the Racecourse/Hyde Park circulars, with High Street to the left and Hall Gate to the right. To the rear is Silver Street, with the building in the previous picture in the distance, as 23 enters Cleveland Street. This vehicle was supplied free in lieu of 22 being loaned for demonstration in Johannesburg in early 1930. It was here where Hyde Park vehicles returning to depot would approach the road junction from the right and then have booms transferred to the Cleveland Street wiring. They then travelled to St Sepulchre Gate to be facing in the right direction for yet another boom change to reach French Gate, or later High Fisher Gate. (J Fordham collection)

46. Continuing towards the town centre, rebodied Sunbeam W 351 (ex Pontypridd 10) turns out of Cleveland Street into Printing Office Street on the last leg of the journey from Wheatley Hills. A superb Jaguar Mk VII, with a Leicester registration, and a Flying Standard on the left, complete the picture.
(R F Mack/J Fozard copyright)

← 47. At the end of Printing Office Street, rebodied Sunbeam W 388 (ex Southend 134) waits to make the turn into St Sepulchre Gate and onto the Beckett Road stand. The nearside wiring can be seen pulled off to the traction standard to the rear of 388. This was used in later years by vehicles entering service on the Balby and Hexthorpe routes. Trolleybuses would leave the depot via High Fisher Gate and Market Place, where wiring allowed movement into Silver Street and thence to Printing Office Street. Boom transfer would occur at the location illustrated in this view and vehicles would then cross to Jacobs Corner to turn into West Laith Gate.
(R F Mack/NTA collection)

← 48. This view illustrates the final manoeuvre described in the previous picture with the booms of rebodied Karrier W 371 about to be transferred to the nearside wiring, thereby providing access to the West Laith Gate stands.
(R F Mack/NTA collection)

49. The final picture in this sequence depicts rebodied Karrier W 376 on the Beckett Road route completing the turn into St Sepulchre Gate, and about to pass under the diamond crossover carrying the Hyde Park wiring in the opposite direction. The access wiring for the Balby and Hexthorpe vehicles taking up service, referred to in Pictures 47/48, can be seen immediately above the Austin A40 saloon leaving the scene on the right. (J Fozard)

RACE COURSE AND HYDE PARK

The Racecourse (destination blinds always showed two words) and Hyde Park routes were circulars operating in opposite directions along the same roads. In following these routes the picture sequence is presented in a clockwise direction, with vehicles depicted travelling in both directions.

50. The Racecourse route operated in a clockwise direction and rebodied Karrier W 369 is seen at the town centre stand in St Sepulchre Gate, complete with Sunbeam badge, in October 1963. The vehicle has been rejuvenated with a modern Roe body, as have the three trolleybuses to the rear. Three sets of overhead wiring are depicted; vehicles on the Beckett Road and Wheatley Hills routes used the centre set. On occasions, Racecourse trolleybuses had to lower booms to allow vehicles on these routes to pass. Those on the right provided two way depot egress and return for the Bentley, Balby/Hexthorpe and Beckett Road/Wheatley Hills vehicles using French Gate. Hyde Park vehicles returning to depot also used this wiring having achieved the right direction as described in Picture 45. (G Warnes)

51. Apart from the normal service to the famous racecourse, numerous specials were provided on meeting days. Here BUT 381 (ex Darlington 71) is seen in the same location as the previous picture, but facing in the opposite direction, ready to enter service on a racecourse special. It has travelled along St Sepulchre Gate on the wrong side of the road against oncoming traffic, as indicated earlier. The next move for 381 will be to cross to the centre of the road to allow booms to be transferred to the fourth set of Hyde Park wiring on the opposite side of the road.
(R F Mack/J Fozard copyright)

52. Racecourse specials assembled in St Sepulchre Gate ready to travel round the anti clockwise Hyde Park route to the meeting venue. Rebodied Sunbeam W 391 (ex Southend 137) leads the line up, and the vehicle seen in the previous picture is on the extreme left. The diamond crossover carrying the wiring from Printing Office Street is top left. (R F Mack/J Fozard copyright)

53. At the Clock Corner, one of the early vehicles, in original livery, turns out of St Sepulchre Gate into High Street and onward to the racecourse in the late afternoon. The centre road is Baxter Gate leading to the Market Place, with a similar vehicle in the far distance on its way to Beckett Road or Wheatley Hills. (J Fordham collection)

54. Travelling in the opposite anti-clockwise direction on the Hyde Park route, rebodied Karrier W 375 moves along High Street towards Clock Corner in June 1955, and is about to turn left into St Sepulchre Gate. On the left, a traditional barber's pole can be seen, plus the Picture House cinema, later to become the ABC. In the far distance is Hall Gate, which 375 has travelled along from the racecourse. (G Warnes)

55. Rebodied Karrier W 376 continues along High Street on the Racecourse circuit in August 1963, passing the imposing building of the then Westminster Bank, with the Clock Corner in the background. The modern vertical light on the left was one of two that provided illumination to the front of the eighteenth century Mansion House; the former clashes somewhat with the adjacent building architecture (A D Packer)

← 56. With the Gaumont cinema on the left, now demolished, rebodied Karrier W 369 has just left South Parade and is about to enter Hall Gate, followed by Vauxhall and Ford saloons. The cinema was subsequently renamed under the Odeon banner. The vehicle livery includes the three white bands applied when first re-entering service, and the road junction was one of the first in the town to be controlled by traffic lights. (S N J White collection)

← 57. Rebodied Karrier W 375 moves along the dual carriageway of Bennetthorpe, which led from South Parade to the racecourse. Modern semi-detached housing forms the backdrop and 375 will shortly travel around a traffic island and return to town via Hyde Park. This was the last trolleybus in service and is now held at the Trolleybus Museum at Sandtoft, North Lincolnshire. (V Nutton/Travel Lens Photographic)

58. Karrier-Clough E6s, 11 from 1929 and 22 from 1930, both in original livery, stand at the end of Bennetthorpe. 22 was demonstrated in Johannesburg in January 1930, and York early in the following year. Note the hand operated semaphore direction indicator.
(P Tuffrey collection)

59. Looking in the opposite direction along Bennetthorpe, Karrier-Clough E6 22 is still in the same location as seen in the previous picture, whilst sister vehicle 20 travels back towards town. It is on the anti-clockwise circuit via Hyde Park, as indicated above the upper rear window. Note the half hearted attempt to cover the abandoned rare centre groove tram track. (P Tuffrey collection)

60. Rebodied Karrier W 369 continues along Bennetthorpe conveying race goers back to the town centre via Hall Gate and High Street. The destination indicator shows "Special" with a "Racecourse" sticker in the nearside windscreen. A second trolleybus can be seen in the right background and horseboxes are parked to the rear.
(R F Mack/J Fozard copyright)

61. Rebodied Karrier W 377 rounds the traffic island at the racecourse to begin the run back to town via Hyde Park. The Racecourse destination indicator will not be changed, and neither will there be a change on vehicles going in the opposite anti-clockwise Hyde Park direction.
(R F Mack/J Fozard copyright)

← 62. Having negotiated the traffic island, rebodied Sunbeam W 385 (ex Southend 131) is seen in Carr House Road, just past a section insulator. The body was subsequently modified and fitted to a Daimler motorbus. Note the advertisement for Zetters Football Pools, where prizes of £20,000 were of major significance in those pre- National Lottery days. The building on the left is the race day police station. (R F Mack/J Fozard copyright)

← 63. Another racecourse special, moving in the anti-clockwise direction to the venue, travels along the dual carriageway of Carr House Road. Rebodied Sunbeam W 352 (ex Pontypridd 11) carries the Racecourse sticker in the windscreen, with a fare of 6d (2.5p). After withdrawal, the body was adapted to fit Daimler motorbus 171. Co-op Branch No 33 is advertising a wide variety of products ranging from Bisto to coal. (R F Mack/J Fozard copyright)

64. Rebodied Karrier W 375 turns out of Carr House Road into Catherine Street, and thence onwards to Spring Gardens, on a return leg to the town centre from Hyde Park. All this area has been redeveloped since the age of the trolleybus.
(V Nutton/Travel Lens Photographic)

65. Also on a return trip from Hyde Park, rebodied Sunbeam W 394 (ex Mexborough and Swinton 2) travels along Spring Gardens having left Catherine Street, which is to the right of the swimming baths that can be seen in the distance. Note the selection of period cars that would look well on the current rally scene. (Travel Lens Photographic)

66. Rebodied Karrier W 375 turns out of Spring Gardens into St Sepulchre Gate, and thence to the stand for the clockwise Racecourse route. In the background is a section insulator/feeder in the overhead. All things leather were sold from the shop on the left. (R H G Simpson)

67. The town centre stand for the Hyde Park route was in St Sepulchre Gate outside the Doncaster Co-operative department store, which was called "The Emporium". Karrier E6 360 is seen on stand ready for another trip around the circular. Note that the booms are fitted with wheel collectors in this September 1951 view, rather than the later carbon insert skates. (R Marshall)

68. Rebodied Karrier W 377 has nearly finished its clockwise circuit and will shortly reach the town centre Racecourse stand further along St Sepulchre Gate. The Co-operative building dominates the background as 377 is about to pass under a crossover, which carried the wiring from Printing House Street for Balby and Hexthorpe vehicles taking up service in West Laith Gate; they travelled from the depot via High Fisher Gate. The diamond crossing, top left, carried wiring from the same location to the stands for Beckett Road and Wheatley Hills.
(R F Mack/J Fozard copyright)

Doncaster Transport Statistics, 1907-47

Year	Trams	Trolley-buses	Double-deck Buses	Single-deck Buses	Mileage	Revenue	Operating Cost	Capital Costs and Income Tax	Passengers	Appropriation Account	
										Credit	Debit
						£	£	£		£	£
1907	25	—	--	--	495,404	12,397	10 859	3,900	2,753,506	—	1,362
1910	25	----	---	---	488,261	15,172	11,186	4,521	3,411,522	—	134
1915	32	—	—	—	598,765	25,348	16,657	5,921	6,609,270	2,855	—
1920	47	—	--	—	693,695	60,192	56,606	8,572	9,550,825	—	4,572
1925	47	---	---	15	1,317,000	99,815	77,929	15,957	11,621,799	11,574	---
1930	18	22	8	31	2,104,466	120,248	97,429	29,573	16,116,180	—	3,112
1935	9	32	14	22	2,290,020	124,333	85,228	38,167	17,732,428	12,665	—
1940	---	44	26	17	2,587,558	169,269	115,730	33,211	24,524,791	21,250	---
1945	---	45	36	20	2,797,754	296,775	186,393	94,578	39,011,653	20,518	---
1947	---	46	39	17	3,397,158	335,498	221,529	64,522	43,786,570	55,591	—

BALBY AND HEXTHORPE
Town Centre to St James's Bridge

69. Karrier E6 353 is on the wrong side of St Sepulchre Gate, under left hand wiring, about to take up service to Balby. Initially, vehicles for Balby and Hexthorpe left the depot in Greyfriars Road, and travelled around the clockwise Racecourse circular to take up service. The booms were then transferred to the route's terminal loop in the southern part of St Sepulchre Gate near Jacobs Corner. First thing in the morning, to avoid the above journey, vehicles would coast, with booms down, across to West Laith Gate from St Sepulchre Gate, or be pushed across the road junction. To overcome the dead mileage, and the unofficial alternative, a direct connection was made from the nearside wiring in this view across to the route stands in West Laith Gate (see Picture 24).
(D A Jones)

← 70. Both the Balby and Hexthorpe routes terminated in the town centre around a single loop, with the stands in West Laith Gate as shown here. Karrier E6 353 is seen again loading for the former destination, with a sister vehicle behind. Both routes shared overhead from here until St James's Bridge was reached. Note the hanging sign for Mazda light bulbs.
(R F Mack/J Fozard copyright)

← 71. This 1946 photograph depicts Karrier W 77 (later renumbered 377), in the as delivered all over chocolate wartime livery, and waiting on the Hexthorpe stand in West Laith Gate. The Park Royal body was built to a relaxed Ministry of Supply specification, which provided upholstered seats as opposed to the wooden slatted variety. The vehicle was rebodied in 1955. (R Marshall)

72. Still in West Laith Gate, rebodied Karrier W 372 is seen awaiting departure to Hexthorpe looking resplendent in the three white band livery. A pre war Karrier E6 destined for Balby is to the rear.
(R Marshall)

73. Further along West Laith Gate, one of the two post war single deck Sunbeam W's purchased from Mexborough and Swinton (18) has departed from the Balby stand in the distance and is now 354 in the Doncaster fleet, having received a new double deck body. It is reported that the single deck bodies were removed at Mexborough and Swinton's depot at Rawmarsh, one being used as a fibreglass workshop. Note the section insulator/feeder supported by the bracket arm, and the multi badged Humber car outside the premises of Needle and Stovin. (R H G Simpson)

← 74. Rebodied Karrier W 376 continues its outward journey along the single loop in West Laith Gate before turning left into West Street. The early rebodied utility vehicles had beading below the lower windows as seen here. With the use of only a single white band above the lower windows, the need for this feature disappeared on later rebuilds. (S Lockwood collection)

75. Rebodied Sunbeam W 390 (ex Southend 136) reaches the end of West Street on the last stage of the terminal loop and is about to turn right into the southern part of St Sepulchre Gate; the turn out of West Laith Gate is in the background. The modern shop on the right seems well stocked with linoleum; a window cleaner's barrow, typical of the immediate post war period, stands on the left. In the distance behind 390 is the Friends Meeting House. (C Carter)

76. On leaving West Street, outward bound vehicles for Balby and Hexthorpe rejoined double overhead wiring. The conductor of Karrier-Clough E6 20 leans out to check that there are no problems when passing under the overhead crossover, with wiring for the beginning of the town centre loop leading off to the right. Traffic in this pre war era warranted a white coated policeman on point duty, with the earlier building on the right hand corner housing the Co-op Café on the upper floors. The Benefit shoe shop on the left completes the picture.
(G H F Atkins/courtesy & © J Banks collection)

77. Rebodied Karrier W 397 (ex Mexborough and Swinton 5) moves along the southern section of St Sepulchre Gate, with Arbitration Street on the right, on an outward trip to Balby. Note the carrier bicycle parked by the side door and the advertisement for the ever present Heinz Baked Beans.
(R F Mack/NTA collection)

Balby

78. Sunbeam W 384 (ex Southend 130) leaves the town centre and moves towards Balby Road, with the St James's Bridge over the East Coast main line on the left, and the church named after the same saint on the right. The vehicle is seen before rebodying by Doncaster carrying its original Brush utility body. On the right is a Humber Snipe saloon. (P Fox collection)

79. Returning to town along Balby Road, Karrier-Clough E6 27 depicts ideal trolleybus operating territory, comprising a long straight road with residential and commercial properties. In this pre war view, note again the destination indicator above the upper rear window and that two vehicle registration numbers are carried. The traction standards are unusual with three differing diameters, the upper one being particularly slender. The garage on the right carries advertisements for Cleveland and Castrol brands. (J Fordham collection)

80. On a wet day in the early 1950s, Karrier E6 364 makes its way along Balby Road into town passing the White Swan Hotel on the corner of Albany Road, which can be seen on the left. The brands on the advertising hoardings have stood the test of time. (R F Mack/J Fozard copyright)

TROLLEY BUS ROUTE No. 10 — BALBY
DONCASTER, West l th Gate, BALBY, Barrel Lane

SUNDAY

Depart West Laith Gate	Depart Barrel Lane
12 00 noon	12 13 p.:
12 06 p.m.	12 19
12 12	12 25
12 19	12 32

then every 6 and 7 min.
until

1 59 p.m.	2 12 p.m
2 05	2 18
2 10	2 23
2 15	2 28

then every 5 mins. until

4 25 p.m.	4 38 p.m.
4 29	4 42
4 34	4 47
4 38	4 51

then every 4 and 5 mins.
until

6 57 p.m.	7 10 p.m.
7 01	7 14
7 04	7 17
7 08	7 21

then every 3 and 4 mins.
until

10 26 p.m.	10 39 p.m.
10 30	10 43

MONDAY TO FRIDAY

Depart West Laith Gate	Depart Barrel Lane
4 35 a.m.	4 48 a.m.
5 00	5 13
5 06	5 19
5 13	5 26

then every 6 and 7 mins.
until

6 40 a.m.	6 53 a.m.
6 43	6 56
6 46	6 59
6 50	7 03

then every 3 and 4 mins.
until

9 00 a.m.	9 13 a.m.
9 05	9 18

then every 5 mins. until

11 50 a.m.	12 03 p.m.
11 54	12 07

then every 3 and 4 mins.
until

10 52 p.m.	11 05 p.m.
10 56	11 09
11 00	11 13

SATURDAY

Depart West Laith Gate	Depart Barrel Lane
4 35 a.m.	4 48 a.m.
5 00	5 13
5 08	5 21

then every 8 and 9 mins.
until

7 00 a.m.	7 13 a.m.
7 05	7 18
7 09	7 22

then every 3 and 4 mins.
until

} 29 a.m.	8 42 a.m.
! 31	8 44
8 34	8 47

then every 2 and 3 mins.
until

5 25 p.m.	5 38 p m.
5 28	5 41
5 31	5 44

then every 3 mins. until

10 55 p.m.	11 08 p.m.
10 58	11 11
11 00	11 13

BALBY ROUTE (No. 10).

Bk up					
Out	In				
1	1				Town (West Laith Gate)
2	2	1½			Balby Bridge
3	3	1½	1½		Balby Church
4	4	2	1½	1½	Barrel Lane

Timetable and Fare Chart 1950

81. In Balby Road, near Burton Avenue, Karrier E6 367 is outward bound running parallel with what appears to be tram track in the roadway. This was one of the twenty vehicles delivered in 1939, with 366 – 368 arriving in the month war broke out. The shop on the right deals in china and floor covering with coco doormats at 3/6d (17.5p). The advertisements on the wall indicate that Doncaster Rovers next home match is with Port Vale; the other suggests "Women aren't Angels", presumably a film on show locally. Balby Road led into High Road and thence to Warmsworth Road. Two authorised extensions led off High Road, one a turning loop round Oliver/Woodfield Roads and Cross Street, and the other along Hall Flat Lane, Springwell Lane and Broomhouse Lane to its junction with Galsworthy Road; neither were built.
(G Warnes)

82. Rebodied Sunbeam W 390 (ex Southend 136) approaches the terminus along Warmsworth Road. Slightly further back on the right is Austen Avenue, which was the site of the original Balby terminus. Vehicles turned left off Warmsworth Road, travelled a short distance along the avenue, before carrying out a reversing turn at the junction with Cedar Road. The extension to the later terminus was erected in 1942 and the earlier reversing arrangement discontinued. (C Carter)

83. The Balby terminus was at the junction with Barrel Lane, a short distance from the current A1(M) motorway. A triangular traffic island was the turning point and rebodied Karrier W 375 has just arrived and discharged its passengers, with another vehicle returning to town in the distance. An extension from this point through Warmsworth to New Edlington was authorised but never built. The length of road where 375 is standing is now filled in. (W A Camwell)

Hexthorpe

84. We now return to where the Balby and Hexthorpe routes parted company. Here we see Sunbeam W 391 (ex Southend 137), with its original Park Royal utility body, leaving St Sepulchre Gate and about to climb the approach to St James's Bridge over the main East Coast railway line. The vehicle was rebodied in 1958. The YMCA building, originally a hospital, is to the right and the hoarding on the left is advertising Smarties, a brand children would recognise today. Note the catenary support of the overhead top right. (P Tuffrey collection)

85. Just a little further on from the previous view, Karrier E6 365 climbs the bridge approach carrying a standing load in September 1954, with two young schoolboys watching progress. The black and white kerbs in the background are a leftover from wartime road markings to aid drivers in the blackout. To assist passengers, loudspeakers were fitted on each deck so that stops could be identified. The Balby town centre stand was in front of that for Hexthorpe, so on occasions vehicles on the latter route would wait at the foot of the bridge to allow the Balby trolleybus to take the lead. (G Warnes)

← 86. At the same location we see the rear of Sunbeam W 386 (ex Southend 132) before rebodying, as it descends the bridge approach to join St Sepulchre Gate. This style of Park Royal utility body was supplied to a number of operators during, and immediately after the war, including Doncaster and the author's hometown of Derby. The new Roe body fitted to this vehicle was, after adaptation, eventually fitted to Daimler motorbus 168. (P Fox collection)

87. Pre war Karrier E6 359 crests St James's Bridge, known locally as Nine Arch Bridge, over the East Coast main line shortly before the former's withdrawal in 1955. Two axle trolleybuses usually operated the Hexthorpe route after their introduction in the mid 1940s. The St James's Church buildings lay to the left. (G Warnes)

88. This view, taken in November 1954, depicts Karrier W 370 in its original utility form nearing the terminus at the end of Urban Road, with Scarll Road on the left. The slender three diameter traction standards are again well illustrated. (G Warnes)

89. Karrier-Clough E6 18 has reached the Hexthorpe terminus, with smartly dressed passengers leaving to mix with equally elegant pedestrians. All are moving in the same direction suggesting there is some special event on The Flatts, also known as The Dell, a recreational area beyond the terminus. 18 is still in its original livery and a full depth horizontal opening window can be seen on the upper deck. (G H F Atkins/courtesy & © John Banks collection)

TROLLEY BUS ROUTE No. 3 — HEXTHORPE
DONCASTER, West Laith Gate, HEXTHORPE

SUNDAY		FRIDAY	
Depart West Laith Gate	Depart Hexthorpe	Depart West Laith Gate	Depart Hexthorpe
12 00 noon	12 10 p.m.	As Monday to Thursday	
12 10 p.m.	12 20	until	
and every 10 mins. until		4 20 p.m.	4 30 p.m.
3 00 p.m.	3 10 p.m.	4 26	4 36
3 06	3 16	4 33	4 43
3 13	3 23	4 40	4 50
3 20	3 30	4 46	4 56
and every 6 and 7 mins. until		and every 6 and 7 mins. until	
6 40 p.m.	6 50 p.m.	6 20 p.m.	6 30 p.m.
6 50	7 00	6 30	6 40
and every 10 mins. until		and every 10 mins. until	
10 10 p.m.	10 20 p.m.	10 40 p.m.	10 50 p.m.
10 20	10 30	10 50	11 00
10 30	10 40	11 00	11 10

MONDAY to THURSDAY		SATURDAY	
Depart West Laith Gate	Depart Hexthorpe	Depart West Laith Gate	Depart Hexthorpe
		as Monday to Thursday	
		until	
5 10 a.m.	5 20 a.m.	9 20 a.m.	9 30 a.m.
5 30	5 40	9 26	9 36
5 50	6 00	9 33	9 43
6 15	6 25	9 40	9 50
6 40	6 50		
6 50	7 00	and every 6 and 7 mins. until	
and every 10 mins. until		10 46 p.m.	10 56 p.m.
10 40 p.m.	10 50 p.m.	10 53	11 03
10 50	11 00	11 00	11 10
11 00	11 10		

HEXTHORPE ROUTE (No. 3) ... ... Fare 1½d.
Book up 1—2.

Timetable and Fare Chart 1950

90. Having completed the move around the turning circle, which used the wide area created by the junction with Greenfield Lane, Karrier W 377, in its original body format, lays over before returning to town. Note how the middle white livery band has been sloped to go over the top of the windscreen, unlike the vehicle in the next picture. (G Warnes)

91. We now return to the town centre to illustrate the wiring in the southern part of St Sepulchre Gate, whereby Balby and Hexthorpe trolleybuses reached their stands in West Laith Gate. The nearside wiring was the initial stretch of terminal overhead for vehicles returning to town. From here, six of the seven vehicles illustrated will round Jacobs Corner to reach their respective stands. Before direct wiring was provided into West Laith Gate for vehicles entering service, this is where booms were transferred, trolleybuses having made the full circuit of the Racecourse route from the depot, arriving from Spring Gardens under the centre set of overhead. The wiring on the left was for Hyde Park trolleybuses leaving town. In the foreground is Sunbeam W 392 (ex Southend 138), which was rebodied in 1958. This is also where Beckett Road and Wheatley Hills vehicles changed booms from the nearside wiring to the central Racecourse overhead, having reversed round Jacobs Corner from West Laith Gate when entering service via French Gate. (P Tuffrey collection)

92. Rebodied Sunbeam W 397 (ex Mexborough and Swinton 5), in a rather dirty condition, rounds Jacobs Corner into West Laith Gate to reach the Balby stand. The Co-op building, with it's "Dancing Nightly" sign, dominates the background on what appears to be a cold wet day. (R F Mack/NTA collection)

Doncaster to keep trolleys
Plan for through service referred back

DONCASTER town council last week referred back to its transport committee a recommendation that the Beckett Road and Hexthorpe trolley bus services should be replaced by a through motor bus service, and an alteration made to two other services at the same time.

The council approved a transport committee recommendation that the undertaking should continue to operate both motor buses and trolley buses and that it should develop larger-capacity vehicles.

The council is to make an offer to Southend Corporation for nine Sunbeam double-decker trolley buses which will become available when Southend's trolley bus abandonment scheme is implemented. The Sunbeams will be used to replace obsolete Doncaster vehicles.

DEPOT AND ACCESS

The trolleybus fleet was housed in the original tram depot in Greyfriars Road, with the electricity generating station on the opposite side of the road. Also on this side, was a small overflow building erected in 1920 to accommodate the expanding tram fleet. No routes passed the depot so the next few views indicate the depot, plus vehicles entering service and returning at the end of shift.

93. This view depicts the depot entrance and main exit (reversing out) into Greyfriars Road with the power station opposite. There are five sets of overhead with access from either French Gate to the left, or in later years via High Fisher Gate at the end of Greyfriars Road to the right. Much boom changing was required for the manoeuvres in and out of the depot, as witnessed by the bamboo retrieval poles hanging on the left hand wall. The lower section of the steel stanchion has been painted black and white, no doubt to assist drivers when reversing out of the depot. Rebodied Karrier W 377 completes the picture. (V Nutton/Travel Lens Photographic)

94. Inside the depot five tracks can be seen with vehicles parked under four of them. The empty track on the left, which passes the bus wash, exits the building via the double doors into Church View (see Picture 97). Black and white painted stanchions appear again, and evidence of tram track can be seen below the vehicles in the centre. The maximum use of advertising space has been utilised on the rear of the vehicle in the foreground. The remaining rebodied vehicles working from left to right are Karrier W 374, Sunbeam W's 353 and 354 (ex Mexborough and Swinton 14/18) and Karrier W 372. (V Nutton/Travel Lens Photographic)

95. Here Karrier W 375 is seen in its original utility format in May 1952 about to take up service on the Wheatley Hills route. The right hand wiring leads out of the depot, and having reversed into Greyfriars Road, booms are being transferred to wiring that leads to the town centre via French Gate. The shirt sleeved driver opening the windscreen suggests a warm day ahead. (R Marshall)

96. Rebodied Karrier W 372 has left the depot to take up service to Balby and has just turned out of Greyfriars Road into French Gate. An unusual feature was the single positive wire (seen top right), used by vehicles travelling to and from the depot along French Gate with a negative wire each side. This must have led to some operational difficulties when trolleybuses travelling in opposite directions met using the common centre wire. On the left is the power station, with the depot building beyond the swimming baths on the right. (P Tuffrey collection)

97. Rebodied Sunbeam W 388 (ex Southend 134) travels along French Gate, past Morris car dealer E W Jackson, to start a shift on the Hexthorpe route. Beyond the Volunteer Inn are the swimming baths seen in the previous picture, with North Bridge to the left. For a period, there was wiring out through the rear of the depot (see Picture 94), which then continued along Church View and Lord Street to join French Gate to the rear of 388; the wiring can just be seen above the pub sign. One of the negative wires from the three wire arrangement, referred to earlier, appears to have been removed by the time this view was taken.
(S Lockwood collection)

➜   98. Road works at the town end of French Gate means BUT 383 (ex Darlington 73) moves along the wrong side of the road to take up service on the Bentley route, closely followed by a Thornycroft lorry. It will continue along French Gate and then turn right into St Sepulchre Gate, travel its length on the wrong side of the road, and then follow the single wiring described in Pictures 3 and 4. (G Warnes)

➜   99. In later years, the depot access via French Gate was abandoned, with trolleybuses leaving the Market Place and travelling along High Fisher Gate to join Greyfriars Road, and thence to the depot from the opposite direction. Initially, there was only single wiring before subsequent doubling and BUT 380 (ex Darlington 70) is seen under the former arrangement as it leaves High Fisher Gate and enters Greyfriars Road, with Hanley's Mill as the backdrop. (P Tuffrey collection)

100. The subsequent doubling of the wiring along High Fisher Gate can be seen in this view. Note how the right hand overhead is suspended from the end of the bracket arm to the traction standard on the right. The picture provides a good selection of period cars and commercial vehicles, including a Commer Superpoise third on the right. Hanley's Mill is in the distance. (P Tuffrey collection)

ROLLING STOCK

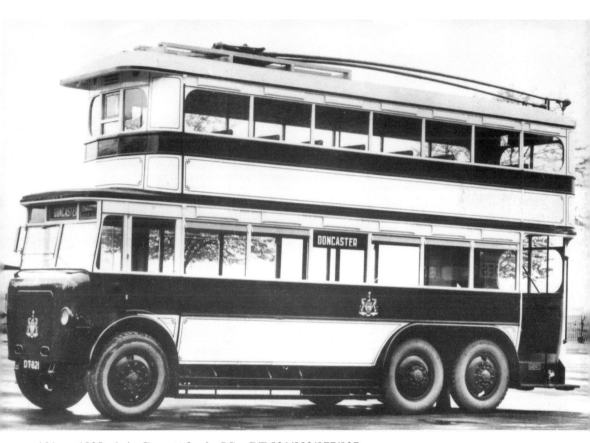

101.   **1928   1-4   Garrett 3axle OS   DT 821/992/977/937**

There is some uncertainty about the registration numbers of 2-4

These initial trolleybuses for the opening of the system were fitted with Bull 60 HP motors and Roe 60 seat bodies. 1 was used for training purposes ready for the conversion (see Picture 1), and also after withdrawal from normal service between June 1936 and July 1938. The remaining three vehicles were withdrawn in 1935/6. Film exists of 1 being demonstrated on the Mexborough and Swinton system in 1929, and is seen here in an official photograph when new.
(R Marshall collection)

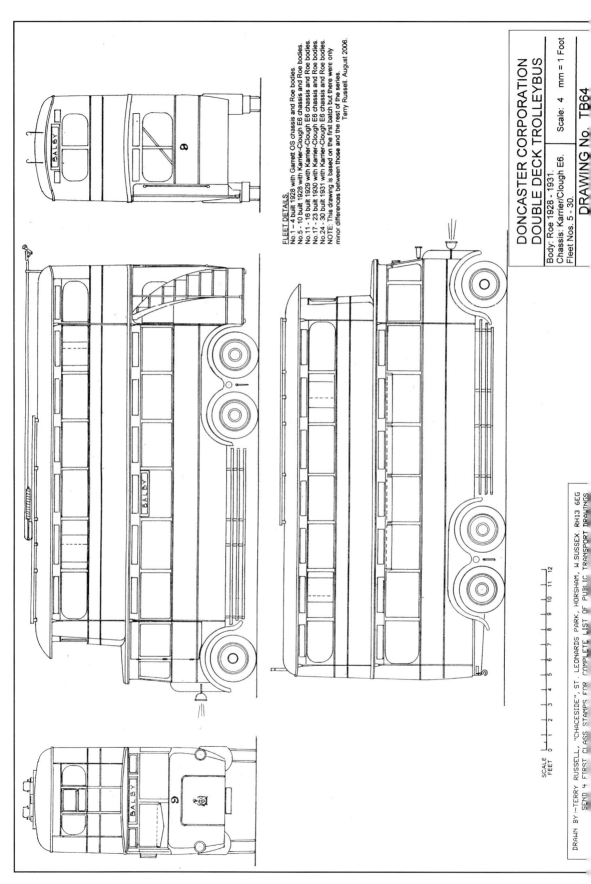

FLEET DETAILS.
No 1 - 4 built 1928 with Garrett OS chassis and Roe bodies.
No 5 - 10 built 1928 with Karrier-Clough E6 chassis and Roe bodies.
No.11 - 16 built 1929 with Karrier-Clough E6 chassis and Roe bodies.
No.17 - 23 built 1930 with Karrier-Clough E6 chassis and Roe bodies.
No.24 - 30 built 1931 with Karrier-Clough E6 chassis and Roe bodies.
NOTE: This drawing is based on the first batch but there were only
minor differences between those and the rest of the series.
Terry Russell. August 2006.

BALBY

DONCASTER CORPORATION
DOUBLE DECK TROLLEYBUS

Body: Roe 1928 - 1931.
Chassis: Karrier/Clough E6.
Fleet Nos. 5 - 30.

Scale: 4 mm = 1 Foot

DRAWING No. TB64

SCALE FEET 0 1 2 3 4 5 6 7 8 9 10 11 12

DRAWN BY:-TERRY RUSSELL, "CHACESIDE", ST. LEONARDS PARK, HORSHAM, W.SUSSEX. RH13 6EG
SEND 4 FIRST CLASS STAMPS FOR COMPLETE LIST OF PUBLIC TRANSPORT DRAWINGS

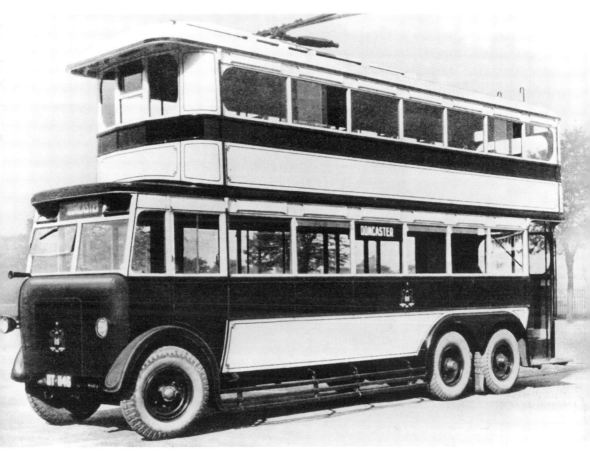

102.	1928	5-10	Karrier-Clough E6	DT1099/1118/1143/1146/1193/1206
	1929	11-16	Karrier-Clough E6	DT1745/1746/1747/1749/1748/1750
	1930	17-23	Karrier-Clough E6	DT2002/2003/2165/2166/2167/2168/2633
	1931	24-30	Karrier-Clough E6	DT3153-3159

These 26 vehicles were all similar with BTH motors (5-23 66HP; 24-30 77HP) and fitted with Roe 60 seat bodies to the same basic design as 1-4. 8, which is illustrated here, was demonstrated to Nottingham City Transport and Mexborough and Swinton in 1930, and 6 loaned to Nottingham. 24-30 had the front destination boxes mounted above the cab roof (see Picture 2). Earliest withdrawal came in 1937, with some of the last three batches lasting into 1945. 17 was exhibited on the Roe stand at Olympia in 1929, and 21 loaned to the BBC for radio interference tests in 1930. 22 was demonstrated to Johannesburg in 1930 and York in 1931. Six or seven of the above vehicles were stored in the Leicester Avenue motorbus depot until the end of 1944 to cover possible war damage to the trolleybus fleet. (S Lockwood collection)

THE

"KARRIER-CLOUGH"

SIX WHEEL TROLLEY OMNIBUS
CHASSIS

Has been selected by the

DONCASTER CORPORATION

for the Conversion of a further Section of their
Tramways System after having operated a fleet
of similar vehicles for over 80,000 bus miles.

Suppliers—

CLOUGH, SMITH & CO. LTD.

36 Victoria Street, Westminster —— LONDON, S.W.1

Telephone No.—VIC. 7937   *Tel. Address*—"CLUFMIT SOWEST LONDON"

103.   Advertisement for the Karrier-Clough trolleybus.

1932 31 Bristol E101 DT 2620

No photograph has been located and there is conflicting information about this vehicle.
The text below is the author's best summary.
This vehicle was a demonstrator built by Bristol Tramways, and it is suggested it started life as a
motorbus chassis and exhibited at the 1929 Commercial Motor Show. There are varying reports
of it being exhibited either as a trolleybus chassis, or in a completed form. It was licensed as a
demonstrator to Doncaster in August 1930, and eventually purchased in early 1932. The 60 seat
body was by Roe, and a BTH motor fitted; withdrawal came in 1945. Only one other Bristol
trolleybus was built, appropriately owned by Pontypridd Urban District Council from whom
Doncaster purchased two vehicles in 1957.

104.   **1934**   **32(332)**   **Karrier E6**   **DT 4718**

This was the first vehicle delivered without a projecting driver's canopy and all subsequent deliveries were flat fronted. The 60 seat body was built by Roe and the motor variously reported as being supplied by BTH (60HP) or Metro-vick (80HP). It is also reported that the chromium plated chassis was exhibited at the 1933 Commercial Motor Show. 300 was added to the fleet number in 1948 and withdrawal came in 1952. 332 is seen here at the North Bridge bus station. (K Bettis)

105. **1935 33-36 (333-336)**
      Karrier E6 DT 5772-5775

106. **1935 37-39 (337-339) Karrier E6 DT 6539-6541**
➜ **1936 40-42 (340-342) Karrier E6 DT 6542-6544**

Roe 60 seat bodies were fitted to these four vehicles to a design similar to that mounted on 32 (332). Metro-vick 80HP motors were installed and the batch was withdrawn between 1952 and 1953. 336 is seen at the North Bridge bus station after renumbering. (R Marshall)

These six vehicles were delivered over the three months covering the year end and were fitted with Roe 60 seat bodies plus 80HP Metro-vick motors. The front had smooth lines with the bulbous lower panel of previous deliveries being dispensed with. 37 was exhibited at the 1935 Commercial Motor Show and the batch was renumbered in 1948; withdrawal came in 1954. 341 awaits departure to Bentley from the North Bridge bus station. (R Marshall)

107. **1938 43-48 (343-348) Karrier E6 ADT 181-186**
➜ **1939 49-68 (349-368) Karrier E6 BDT 114-129/131-134**

Karrier was again specified for the last pre war deliveries and fitted with Metro-vick 85HP motors and Roe 60 seat bodies. 300 was added to the fleet numbers in 1948 and 362 loaned to Rotherham Corporation in 1955 for checking height clearances under the overhead wiring prior to the introduction of double deck trolleybuses in the town. First withdrawals came in 1954, and all had succumbed by 1957. 353 is seen outside the depot in May 1952. (R Marshall)

108. **1944 69-71 (369-371) Karrier W CDT 312-314 Park Royal Utility Body**
      1945 72-74 (372-374) Karrier W CDT 624-626 Brush Utility Body
      1945 75-77 (375-377) Karrier W CDT 636-638 Park Royal Utility Body

These nine vehicles were built to a wartime Ministry of Supply utility specification, hence the W reference in the chassis designation. The chassis were built at Sunbeam's Wolverhampton factory but badge engineered to carry the Karrier name, thus reflecting Doncaster's pre war deliveries. All had Metro-vick 85HP motors, 56 seat bodies and were renumbered in the 300 series in 1948. 69-71 were delivered at the end of 1943 and entered service in 1944 being fitted with upholstered seats and painted grey. Roe rebodied them between 1955 and 1958 incorporating 62 seats. 72-77 received relaxed Ministry Mark 2 bodies with upholstered seats, rounded roof dome, additional opening windows and painted in an all over chocolate livery; all were fitted with new Roe 62 seat bodies in 1954/55. The new body of 370 was eventually fitted to a Daimler motorbus. 375 made the last journey at the closure of the system on 14th December 1963. 370, typical of the Park Royal bodied vehicles, is seen in Greyfriars Road outside the depot; a rebodied vehicle from this batch can be seen in Picture 30. An example of the Brush bodied batch can be seen in Picture 24. (P Yeomans)

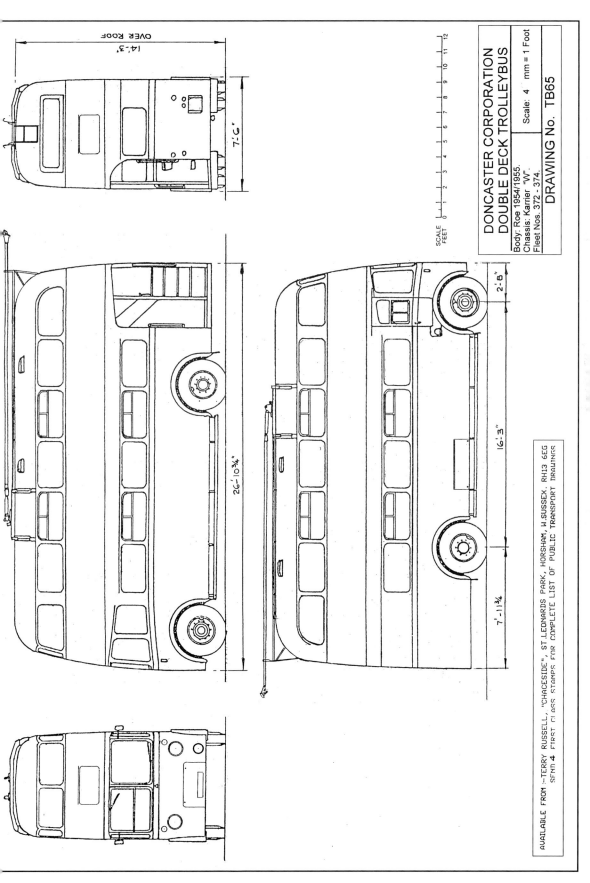

OVER ROOF

14'-3"

7'-6"

26'-10¾"

16'-3"

2'-8"

7'-11¾"

SCALE
FEET

0 1 2 3 4 5 6 7 8 9 10 11 12

DONCASTER CORPORATION
DOUBLE DECK TROLLEYBUS

Scale: 4 mm = 1 Foot

Body: Roe 1954/1955.
Chassis: Karrier "W".
Fleet Nos. 372 - 374.

DRAWING No. TB65

AVAILABLE FROM :-TERRY RUSSELL, "CHACESIDE", ST LEONARDS PARK, HORSHAM, W.SUSSEX. RH13 6EG
SEND 4 FIRST CLASS STAMPS FOR COMPLETE LIST OF PUBLIC TRANSPORT DRAWINGS

All post war purchases were second hand from a variety of sources. After overhaul, the majority were rebodied, some entering service with Doncaster before receiving new bodies. After withdrawal, a number had the bodies adapted to fit motorbuses. One batch of second hand trolleybuses was sold on to a third operator in their original condition.

109.　　**1952　378-383　BUT 9611T　LHN 780-785**

The first six second hand vehicles were purchased from Darlington Corporation (68-73) where they had entered service in 1949. Powerful EEC 120HP motors were fitted, together with 56 seat East Lancashire bodies. Emergency traction batteries were carried until 1956. The vehicles had been purchased by Darlington based on a promise the Council would lower the road under railway bridges on the Harrowgate Hill to Lingfield Lane route. Nothing happened and the double deckers were relegated to routes where the indigenous single deck vehicles would suffice. Given the impending trolleybus replacement programme, the three year old vehicles were put up for sale to maximise value, and purchased by Doncaster in 1952. They were withdrawn in 1959 and sold to Bradford City Transport, with 378 being cannibalised for spares, and the remaining five rebodied by Bradford with East Lancashire 66 seat front entrance 8ft (2.44m) wide bodies, becoming 831-835 in their fleet. 834 is held at the Trolleybus Museum at Sandtoft. 378 is seen here when in the Darlington fleet, numbered 68, and waiting in Prebend Row. These were the only UK trolleybuses to be operated by three different municipalities. Picture 8 depicts a vehicle from this batch when in the Doncaster fleet. (H Luff/OTA/Photobus)

| 110. | 1954 | 384 | Sunbeam W BHJ 827 | Brush Utility Body |
| | | 385-392 | Sunbeam W BHJ 828-829/898-903 | Park Royal Utility Body |

The next nine second hand purchases were from Southend Corporation. All were fitted with BTH 85HP motors and 56 seat bodies to relaxed wartime Ministry specification. They were numbered 130-138 in the Southend fleet, and purchased by them in 1945/46. All entered service with Doncaster in 1954, and received new Roe 62 seat bodies between 1957 and 1959. After withdrawal in 1961/62, the bodies were converted to half cab configuration and fitted to Daimler motorbus chassis. 386 is seen when operating in Southend as their 132 on what appears to be an enthusiasts' special. To see a vehicle from this batch in Doncaster's service, refer to Pictures 62 and 91; the single Brush bodied example can be seen in Picture 78.

(R F Mack/NTA collection)

111. **1954   393-398**
      Sunbeam W
      EWT 478-480/513-515

These six vehicles were wartime single deck utility trolleybuses delivered to Mexborough and Swinton in 1943, and numbered 1-6 in their fleet. They were acquired by Doncaster in 1954, and the original Brush utility bodies replaced by new Roe 62 seat double deck bodies before entering service. BTH 85HP motors were fitted and after withdrawal in 1962/63 they were converted to half cab configuration and mounted on Leyland motorbus chassis. Mexborough 2 (Doncaster 394) is seen on home territory in Frederick Street, Rotherham loading for the route to Rawmarsh via Green Lane. Picture 26 depicts 397 from the batch in its double deck format when with Doncaster.
(D A Jones)

112. **1957   351-352**
➔   **Karrier W   FNY 983-984**

Pontypridd Urban District Council was the source of the next two trolleybuses, being 10/11 in their fleet and delivered to them in 1944. They had EEC 80HP motors, automatic acceleration, and Weymann wartime utility bodies that were replaced by new Roe 62 seat versions when acquired by Doncaster in 1957. 351 had the acceleration feature removed in 1960 and a Metro-vick 85HP motor fitted. The Weymann utility bodies always looked narrower than their Park Royal counterparts. When withdrawn in 1962, they also had bodies modified to fit Daimler motorbus chassis. 10 (Doncaster 351) is seen here on home ground crossing the newer Victoria Bridge over the River Taff; the earlier Old Bridge, also know as William Edwards Bridge or Pontypridd Bridge, is to the right. Note the pre war Packard car to the rear. For a view of 351 in Doncaster rebodied form see Picture 27. (R Marshall)

113. 1958   353-354   Sunbeam W   FWX 898/902

The final two secondhand vehicles were also from Mexborough and Swinton and numbered 14/18 in their fleet. They were delivered in 1947 and were fitted with BTH 85HP motors and 32 seat post war single deck central entrance Brush bodies. Acquired by Doncaster in 1957 in chassis only format, they received new 62 seat double deck Roe bodies, which in turn were modified to fit Leyland motorbus chassis after withdrawal in 1963. 14 (Doncaster 353) is depicted with its original owner in May 1954 and can be seen in its rejuvenated form in Picture 94. (A D Packer)

Thus the last nineteen trolleybus bodies built for mounting on second hand vehicles saw further service on motorbus chassis after the closure of the electric system. This would suggest very astute forward planning, which maximised the return on the initial capital investment.

TOWER WAGONS

➔ 114. There were four motorised tower wagons over the life of both the tramway and trolleybus systems. The first was an Albion G (C 6407), which covered both systems, with the tower being subsequently transferred to two later vehicles, namely Bristol 4 ton WY 5608 in 1928 (ex bus 1), and then Leyland TS7 DT 7617 in 1950. A dedicated tower wagon was purchased in 1946, namely Karrier EDT 21. The Leyland TS7 was converted from 1936 single deck motorbus 7, and is depicted here outside the depot in Greyfriars Road. In its earlier life, it was converted to an ambulance from 1939 to 1945 and returned to service with Doncaster in 1946, before the later conversion to a tower wagon. (R F Mack/NTA collection)

← 115. Tower wagons and linesmen at work in February 1958. The location is the Beckett Road terminal loop, with the overhead being erected for the extension from the second Parkway terminus. The rear vehicle is the Karrier, with the Leyland TS7 immediately in front. The lorry is a wartime Guy Vixen (CDT 393), which is carrying the large drum of wire to be played out to the linesmen on the two tower wagons. In nearly six years time this installation would be removed after the closure of the system. (R Holmes)

LOAN ASSIGNMENT

116. Rotherham Corporation operated single deck trolleybuses from the opening of the system in October 1912, but to improve revenue it was decided in 1955 a number of post war Daimler trolleybuses should to be rebuilt into double deck format. It was felt necessary to check the height clearances under the Rotherham overhead and Doncaster's Karrier E6 362 was borrowed on 19th June for this task. 362 is seen here in Frederick Street, Rotherham, to the rear of Mexborough and Swinton Sunbeam F4 33, which had run into the town from the north. A tower wagon is in close attendance behind. The photographer followed 362 from Doncaster to Rotherham on his bicycle in order to take a number of pictures of this event. This included an invitation from Rotherham's manager to take views in the depot yard after realising no official record of the trials had been included in the schedule. (G Warnes)

LAST DAY

117. As the change to motor buses progressed only one trolleybus, namely 375, was in service immediately prior to the closure of the system on 14th December 1963. This vehicle was used for the last public journey, with souvenir tickets being issued and it carried a between decks poster indicating "1928 – 1963 Doncaster's Last Trolley Bus". The crew comprised Driver Stanley Frith and Conductor Horace Bowers, and after the last public journey, a final trip was made carrying council officials and long service employees, after which 375 made its way back to Greyfriars Road. The vehicle was donated to the Doncaster Omnibus and Light Railway Society for preservation. After a period of outside storage at Stainforth, it was transferred to the Trolleybus Museum at Sandtoft where it now resides. Here 375 awaits departure in Printing Office Street for one of the last two journeys. So ended over 61 years of electrically powered public transport in the town; trolleybuses contributed just over 35 years. (J Copeland)

THE AFTER LIFE

← 118. After Karrier W 375 completed the last journey in Doncaster, it is seen here operating again at the Trolleybus Museum at Sandtoft, North Lincolnshire resplendent in lined out livery, and carrying passengers around the museum circuit. (D F Parker)

← 119. This view depicts motorbus Leyland PD2/1 94, originally purchased in 1947, after being fitted with the body from trolleybus 393 following the latter's withdrawal in 1963. Roe converted the body to half cab layout and the total life of the structure over its two host chassis was 18 years, which proved a very wise investment. This vehicle can also be seen at Sandtoft. (P Sykes/OTA)

120. Darlington BUT 73 (Doncaster 383) is seen here with its third owner, Bradford City Transport. After being purchased from Doncaster, Bradford fitted a new front entrance body built by East Lancashire Coachbuilders in 1962. Now numbered 835 in the new owner's fleet, the BUT turns round the traffic island at Town Hall Square. This vehicle lasted nine years in this format so the original chassis lasted twenty two years, after allowing for reconditioning. 835 is privately owned and currently resides in the Stagecoach South Shields depot. A view of 383 in Doncaster can be seen in Picture 98. (D F Parker)

MP Middleton Press

EVOLVING THE ULTIMATE RAIL ENCYCLOPEDIA

Easebourne Lane, Midhurst, West Suss
GU29 9AZ   Tel:01730 813169
email:info@middletonpress.co.uk

ISBN PREFIXES - A-978 0 906520 B- 978 1 873793 C- 978 1 901706 D-978 1 904474 E - 978 1 906008

* BROCHURE AVAILABLE SHOWING RAILWAY ALBUMS AND NEW TITLES *

ORDER ONLINE - *PLEASE VISIT OUR WEBSITE* - www.middletonpress.co.u

TRAMWAY CLASSICS *Editor Robert J Harley*

Aldgate & Stepney Tramways to Hackney and West India Docks	B 70 1
Barnet & Finchley Tramways to Golders Green and Highgate	B 93 0
Bath Tramways Peter Davey and Paul Welland	B 86 2
Blackpool Tramways 1933-66 75 years of Streamliners Stephen Lockwood	E 34 5
Bournemouth & Poole Tramways Roy C Anderson	B 47 3
Brighton's Tramways The Corporation's routes plus lines to Shoreham and Rottingdean	B 02 2
Bristol's Tramways A massive system radiating to ten destinations Peter Davey	B 57 2
Burton & Ashby Tramways An often rural light railway Peter M White	C 51 2
Camberwell & West Norwood Trys including Herne Hill and Peckham Rye	B 22 0
Chester Tramways Barry M Marsden	E 04 8
Chesterfield Tramways a typical provincial system Barry Marsden	D 37 1
Clapham & Streatham Tramways including Tooting and Earlsfield J.Gent & J.Meredith	B 97 8
Croydon's Tramways including Crystal Palace, Mitcham and Sutton JB Gent & JH Meredith	B 42 8
Derby Tramways a comprehensive city system Colin Barker	D 17 3
Dover's Tramways from River and Maxton	B 24 4
East Ham & West Ham Trys from Stratford and Ilford down to the docks	B 52 7
Edgware & Willesden Tramways including Sudbury, Paddington & Acton	C 18 5
Embankment & Waterloo Trys including the fondly remembered Kingsway Subway	B 41 1
Exeter & Taunton Tramways Two charming small systems J B Perkin	B 32 9
Fulwell - Home for Trams, Trolleys and Buses Professor Bryan Woodriff	D 11 1
Gosport & Horndean Tramways Martin Petch	B 92 3
Great Yarmouth Tramways A seaside pleasure trip Dave Mackley	D 13 5
Hammersmith & Hounslow Trys branches to Hanwell, Acton & Shepherds Bush	C 33 8
Hampstead & Highgate Trys from Tottenham Court Road and Kings Cross Dave Jones	B 53 4
Hastings Tramways Seafront joys and rural trips	B 18 3
Holborn & Finsbury Tramways Angel-Balls Pond Road - Moorgate - Bloomsbury	B 79 4
Huddersfield Tramways the original municipal system Stephen Lockwood	D 95 1
Hull Tramways Level crossings and bridges abound Paul Morfitt & Malcolm Wells	D 60 9
Ilford & Barking Tramways to Barkingside, Chadwell Heath and Beckton	B 61 9
Ilkeston & Glossop Tramways Barry M Marsden	D 40 1
Ipswich Tramways Colin Barker	E 55 0
Keighley Tramways & Trolleybuses Barry M Marsden	D 83 8
Kingston & Wimbledon Trys incl Hampton Court, Tooting & four routes from Kingston	B 56 5
Liverpool Tramways - 1 Eastern Routes	C 04 8
Liverpool Tramways - 2 Southern Routes	C 23 9
Liverpool Tramways - 3 Northern Routes triliogy by Brian Martin	C 46 8
Llandudno & Colwyn Bay Tramways Stephen Lockwood	E 17 8
Lowestoft Tramways a seaside system David Mackley	E 74 1
Maidstone & Chatham Trys from Barming to Loose and from Strood to Rainham	B 40 4
Margate & Ramsgate Tramways including Broadstairs	C 52 9
North Kent Tramways including Bexley, Erith, Dartford, Gravesend and Sheerness	B 44 2
Norwich Tramways A popular system comprising ten main routes David Mackley	C 40 6
Nottinghamshire & Derbyshire Try including the Matlock Cable Tramway Barry M Marsden	D 53 1
Portsmouth Tramways including Southsea Martin Petch	B 72 5

Reading Tramways Three routes - a comprehensive coverage Edgar Jordon	B
Scarborough Tramway including the Scarborough Cliff Lifts Barry M Marsden	E
Seaton & Eastbourne Tramways	B
Shepherds Bush & Uxbridge Tramways including Ealing John C Gillham	C
South London Tramways 1903-33 Wandsworth - Dartford	D
South London Tramways 1933-52 The Thames to Croydon	D
Southampton Tramways Martin Petch	B
Southend-on-Sea Tramways including the Pier Electric Railway	B
Southwark & Deptford Tramways including the Old Kent Road	B
Stamford Hill Tramways including Stoke Newington and Liverpool Street	B
Twickenham & Kingston Trys extending to Richmond Bridge and Wimbledon	C
Victoria & Lambeth Tramways to Nine Elms, Brixton and Kennington	B
Waltham Cross & Edmonton Trys to Finsbury Park, Wood Green and Enfield	C
Walthamstow & Leyton Trys including Clapton, Chingford Hill and Woodford	B
Wandsworth & Battersea Trys from Hammersmith, Putney and Chelsea	B
York Tramways & Trolleybuses Barry M Marsden	D

TRIUMPHANT TRAMWAYS *FULL COLOUR THROUGHOUT*

Triumphant Tramways - England Stephen Lockwood	E

Blackpool * Croydon * Manchester * Midland Metro * Nottingham * Sheffield

TROLLEYBUSES *(all limp covers)*

Birmingham Trolleybuses ... David Harvey	E
Bournemouth Trolleybuses ... Malcolm N Pearce	C
Bradford Trolleybuses ... Stephen Lockwood	D
Brighton Trolleybuses ... Andrew Henbest	D
Cardiff Trolleybuses ... Stephen Lockwood	D
Chesterfield Trolleybuses ... Barry M Marsden	D
Croydon Trolleybuses ... Terry Russell	B
Darlington Trolleybuses ... Stephen Lockwood	D
Derby Trolleybuses ... Colin Barker	C
Doncaster Trolleybuses ... Colin Barker	E
Grimsby & Cleethorpes Trolleybuses ... Colin Barker	D
Huddersfield Trolleybuses ... Stephen Lockwood	C
Hull Trolleybuses ... Paul Morfitt and Malcolm Wells	D
Ipswich Trolleybuses ... Colin Barker	D
Mexborough & Swinton Trolleybuses ... Colin Barker	E
Newcastle Trolleybuses ... Stephen Lockwood	D
Nottinghamshire & Derbyshire Trolleybuses ... Barry M Marsden	D
Reading Trolleybuses ... David Hall	C
South Shields Trolleybuses ... Stephen Lockwood	E
Tees-side Trolleybuses ... Stephen Lockwood	D
Wolverhampton Trolleybuses 1961-67 ... Graham Sidwell	D
Woolwich and Dartford Trolleybuses ... Robert J Harley	B